"D'vorah Lansky has simplified the mystifying world of virtual book tours with a practical, step-by-step, plan for finding blog hosts, communicating with them, and creating content."

Mal Duane, best-selling author of *Alpha Chick: Five Steps for Moving from Pain to Power* , AlphaChick.com

"A virtual book tour provides authors with exposure they simply would not be able to achieve with the 'old-school,' in-person book signings. D'vorah is a pioneer and expert on virtual book tours for authors. She has a wealth of information to share."

Della Bercovitch, co-owner, Book Marketing Services BookMarketingServices.org

I0115861

21 Ways to Launch a Successful Virtual Book Tour

21 WAYS

to launch a
successful
virtual book tour

D'vorah Lansky, M.Ed.

Vibrant Marketing Publications
Hartford, CT

Published by Vibrant Marketing Publications
Copyright ©2013 D'vorah Lansky

VibrantMarketingPublications.com

ISBN 978-1-947158-14-6

Dedication

This book is dedicated to my brother David, who has accomplished great things as he's worked toward his dream of land ownership.

David, you have given selflessly to your community through your *Computer Placement Services* program. Hundreds of seniors and school-age children now have affordable computers because of you.

Believe in your dream, Bro, the way I believe in you! Here's to dreams coming true!

Thank you to the hundreds of students who have gone through the Virtual Book Tours Made Easy program. Your enthusiastic participation has provided the foundation for this book.

To our first Virtual Book Tours Hall of Fame achievers: Jo Ann Kairys, Mal Duane, Kate Loving Shenk, Moreen Torpy, Helen Le Mesurier and Jordan Gray, I'm thrilled to be on this success journey with you!

Introduction

A virtual book tour is much like a traditional book tour, but instead of authors traveling from city to city and venue to venue, hoping there will be a crowd when they arrive, they travel virtually to a variety of targeted blogs across the Internet.

During your virtual book tour, you have the opportunity to be hosted by experts in your industry who help to promote you and introduce you to their readers. In this way, you gain credibility and your book is exposed to many new audiences. Your virtual book tour is a powerful way to develop your author platform while introducing yourself to thousands of potential new readers.

As you travel from blog to blog, you share your message in the form of written blog posts. You may also want to add a multimedia component to your virtual book tour by sharing content in audio or video format.

In *21 Ways to Launch a Successful Virtual Book Tour*, you have access to a blueprint for conducting your own virtual book tour. While the 21 "Ways" are provided in sequential order, each "Way" is designed to stand on its own as an effective virtual book tour strategy.

As you dive in, you'll find bite-sized strategies that provide you with king-size results. Take action and you will gain credibility and exposure to new audiences as you take your book on the virtual road!

At the end of each "Way" you'll find suggested action steps. Take time to go through these exercises as you prepare for your own virtual book tour.

Get yourself a dedicated notebook so you can keep track of everything in one handy location. You'll be glad you did.

~ D'vorah

Notes

Notes

Notes

Notes

Notes

_____

_____

_____

_____

_____

_____

_____

_____

_____

_____

_____

_____

_____

_____

_____

_____

_____

WAY 1

Identify Your
Target Audience

The primary activity of a virtual book tour is to "travel" from blog to blog, where you contribute blog posts as a guest blogger. Participating in a virtual book tour increases your credibility as you share your expertise and are endorsed by blog owners. You receive increased visibility and come— by association—to be seen as an expert.

The best blogs to travel to are those that attract your ideal reader. To make the most of this opportunity, you'll want to be clear about who the audience for your book is. This focus is an essential component of your virtual book tour, because knowing who your target audience is helps you to identify and locate blogs and blog owners that attract readers who are interested in your topic or genre. Additionally, this approach provides you with an emphasis as you begin to generate content for your virtual book tour. Getting your message in front of your target audience and those who serve them positions you for increased book sales and speaking opportunities.

Let's say you're a professional organizer who writes on the topic of maximizing the space inside homes. Your target audience could be homeowners. By reaching out to others who serve your target audience, such as realtors, home organizers, virtual organizers, companies that sell organizing materials, and authors who write on the topic of keeping organized, you have the opportunity to reach not only individual homeowners but also professionals who have access to a large number of homeowners.

One of the best ways to connect with your target audience and those who serve them is by joining active and relevant groups on Facebook or LinkedIn. Focus on building relationships, answering and asking questions, and helping others. This strategy will increase your credibility, allow you to make connections, and shine the light on you as an expert.

By establishing relationships with your target audience and those who serve them, you'll develop opportunities to become a guest blogger on a number of highly targeted blogs, creating a win/win/win situation. You gain exposure to new audiences, the blog owners have access to relevant content for their readers, and blog visitors benefit from relevant information of interest to them.

As mentioned in the Introduction, you'll find Action Steps at the end of each "Way." I recommend that you get a dedicated notebook so you can keep track of these action steps for your own virtual book tour.

Action Step: Spend time identifying your target audience

✓ Give thought to which individuals or groups of people would be most interested in or best served by having access to your book and area of expertise. (This is your target audience.)

✓ Which professions, professionals, and/or bloggers serve your target audience?

✓ List the names of people you know who have connections with your target audience or those who serve them.

Notes

WAY 2

Select Your Virtual Book Tour Format

There are several different types of virtual book tour formats to consider. Following are three popular formats from which you can choose to help you get started.

One-Day Teleseminar Virtual Book Tour

The one-day teleseminar is where you speak about your book, via a conference call, for sixty to ninety minutes. You can conduct your teleseminar in an interview format or you may want to share content in more of a book talk or book study format. Having a leader or well-known person in your industry interview you will increase your attendance and credibility.

With the one-day teleseminar, you get the word out to your community and your colleagues can then extend an invitation to their communities. You can also record your talk and have it available for replay. In essence, you're creating a big celebration. This format can be a lot of fun and is a great way to get your message out across the airwaves.

One-Day Blog Blitz Virtual Book Tour

Another virtual book tour format is called the one-day blog blitz. This is an exciting and concentrated way to conduct a virtual book tour. However, it takes a tremendous amount of energy and organization. First, you must write multiple blog posts for all the sites your blitz will appear on. Then you can either coordinate on your own or with your virtual team to get your content to each of the blog owners, and ask the blog owners schedule your posts to appear their sites on the same date.

This format will create a lot of buzz about your book on a given day, and it's an excellent strategy to coordinate during a book launch. Over the course of one day you travel from site to site, thanking your tour hosts and responding to people's comments.

Multi-Day, Multi-Blog Virtual Book Tour

The format I prefer is called the multi-day, multi-blog virtual book tour. This is where you decide on a time frame for your tour, as well as how many days per week you'll be touring during that time frame.

For a first tour, making between six and twelve tour stops is both manageable and effective. For example, let's say you decide to conduct a nine-day virtual book tour and that your tour will take place three days a week for three weeks. You block out these dates on your calendar. As you line up tour hosts, you have a convenient way to track which blog you will be traveling to on which date.

I find this format to be the most effective and relaxed. It also provides prolonged exposure to you and your book and builds momentum over time.

Action Steps: Select your virtual book tour format and schedule your dates

✓ Decide on your virtual book tour format.

✓ If you plan on going with the one-day blog blitz or multi-day, multi-blog virtual book tour format, decide on how many blogs you will tour to.

✓ If you plan on going with the teleseminar format or you'd like to add a multimedia component to your virtual book tour, give thought to who you'd like to have interview you. Jot down their names in your virtual book tour notebook while it's on your mind.

Notes

WAY 3

Develop an Action Plan

It takes time to put all the pieces of your virtual book tour in place. By planning ahead and segmenting your projects, you can effectively accomplish a great deal in the most relaxed way possible.

Give yourself time to prepare

You can pull together a virtual book tour in as little as eight weeks. However, it's advisable to begin planning at least three or four months in advance. That way you'll have plenty of time to:

✓ Identify your target audience

✓ Set up or update your blog

✓ Build relationships with potential hosts

27

- ✓ Line up tour hosts

- ✓ Prepare content

- ✓ Promote your tour

- ✓ Interact with readers

- ✓ Map Out Your Schedule

When planning out your tour, be sure to select a time frame that will allow you to be available to promote your tour and interact with readers. While the majority of the work is done in the months leading up to the tour, you will still need to make sure "all systems are go" and be available to answer comments and questions as you travel from blog to blog.

Rather than focusing on several activities at the same time, consider segmenting your projects. This tactic provides for an enjoyable virtual book tour journey and allows you to achieve a great deal in concentrated blocks of time.

An example of a virtual book tour timeline:

Month One

- ✓ Identify your target audience

- ✓ Set up or update your blog

- ✓ Locate and interact with relevant groups on Facebook and/or LinkedIn

- ✓ Begin making a master list of potential blog hosts

Month Two

✓ Set your virtual book tour dates

✓ Begin scheduling hosts

✓ Send hosts a handwritten thank-you note and a printed or digital copy of your book

✓ Keep track of the details on your calendar, on your virtual book tour tracking sheet, or in your dedicated virtual book tour notebook

Month Three

✓ Block out two weeks to focus on creating the content for your virtual book tour

✓ Create a file with a 100-word signature template you can copy and paste at the end of each of your blog posts

✓ Get your content to each tour host and have them schedule your post

✓ Have each tour host send you the URL of the scheduled post

Month Four

✓ Conduct your virtual book tour

✓ Create a blog post for each day for *your* blog, letting people know where you will be that day (you can pre-schedule your posts to release each day)

✓ Promote your tour stops on social networks

✓ Visit each tour stop to interact and share comments

Reap the rewards

A virtual tour gives you a lot of exposure for your book, now and in the future. By mapping out your schedule and segmenting your activities, you'll efficiently accomplish a great deal, have the opportunity to interact with readers, and enjoy your virtual book tour journey.

Action Step: Develop your action plan

✓ Block out your virtual book tour plan.

✓ Schedule the actual dates for your tour.

✓ Plug your virtual book tour activities into your calendar.

WAY 4

Prepare Your Book Blog

An important aspect of your virtual book tour is that you have an attractive and branded blog dedicated to your book or work. Your blog is the hub of your online world and provides a platform from which you can share your message, sell your products, and build a community. Your blog is not just where people go for content; it's where they go to connect with you.

One way to create an attractive looking blog is to use a premium WordPress theme such as the ones offered by Studio Press. Studio Press themes allow for customization along with access to a supportive members forum.

Prepare the key pages for your book blog:

About Page

The about page is where people can find out more about you and your book. Display a professional headshot photo, with you smiling, prominently on the page. This will provide a powerful visual and allow people to connect with you. Provide a brief bio about you as well as a synopsis of your book.

Blog Page

The blog page is where your blog posts show up. Typically, the newest posts go to the top of the page. The formula for an effective blog post is:

- ✓ A title that includes keywords related to your industry
- ✓ An informative or entertaining article
- ✓ An attractive image
- ✓ A compelling question that engages the reader
- ✓ And a 100-word signature section with one URL, which is added to the end of each blog post.

Contact Page

The contact page gives your audience a way to directly reach you. Rather than listing your email address on the page, I recommend that you add a contact form. This will protect you from receiving spam and will encourage only serious questions and inquiries. One of the easiest ways to add a contact form is with the Contact Buddy WordPress plugin from iThemes.

The Endorsements Page

Your endorsements page is where you can feature recommendations from experts in your field as well as testimonials and book reviews from your readers. For added credibility, include the image of the person giving the endorsement or testimonial. List his or her name, credentials, and the URL to his or her website.

Events Page

Having a schedule of events page provides an easy way for your audience to connect with you and learn more about you and your book. You can include details about upcoming in-person events, such as book signings, as well as virtual events, such as your virtual book tour and virtual speaking engagements. Make sure to include easy-to-access details to encourage audience participation. By doing so, your audience will be able to click on links to your tour stops, follow you on your journey, and interact with new audiences.

Media Page

Your media page is where people go to access your photo, images of your book cover, your author bio, a proposed list of interview questions, and other useful data. Your media page can also provide links to previous interviews and blog posts, newspaper and magazine articles, speaking engagements, online articles, press releases, and more.

Action Step: Streamline your book blog

✓ Head over to your blog and view it from the eyes of your potential book buyers. Be sure that your site is attractive and welcoming and is clear as to what the focus of your site is.

✓ Using the "page" examples listed in this Way, update your site so your readers have easy access to you and your book.

✓ Make sure that it's clear how people can contact you.

WAY **5**

Grow an Ongoing Relationship with Your Audience

As part of your virtual book tour, people will visit your blog. An effective way to grow your business and relationships with your blog visitors is to have a way for them to subscribe to your email list via an opt-in form on your site. You can offer your readers a special report, chapter of your book, or access to an audio recording in exchange for their name and email address. By subscribing to your list, people are giving you permission to communicate with them.

Having an email list is a great way to communicate with and educate your readers. Automating your email communication allows you to streamline your efforts and multiply your results. Not only can you provide your new subscribers with access to the gift you've promised, but you also have a way to communicate easily with them on an ongoing basis. Provide valuable content to your subscribers approximately once per week on topics in which they're interested and give them the opportunity to get to know you.

Provide easy access to your gift

Your opt-in form can be displayed on the left-hand or right-hand side of your blog. We call this location the sidebar. Your email marketing service will provide you with the code needed to create this opt-in form. Typically, you'll find a wide variety of opt-in form designs from which to choose. This will allow you to carry your branded colors through to your opt-in form.

You'll need to have a way for your subscribers to receive their gift. A simple solution is to create a hidden page on your blog that doesn't show up on your navigation bar. Add a thank-you message and a link to your gift and save the page. Next, view this page and copy the URL from the address bar. This is the URL that you'll want to paste into your thank-you email.

Then, when people receive your email, they'll be able to click on the URL to access their gift. There are many email service providers from which to choose. AWeber (AWeber.com) is considered to be one of the best email marketing companies, and it's reputed to have the highest email deliverability rate in the industry. You can have unlimited lists and they provide excellent customer support.

Action Step: Add an Opt-In Form to your blog

✓ Decide what you'll offer to your readers in exchange for their names and email addresses.

✓ Register with an email provider and add an opt-in form to your blog.

✓ Create a hidden page on your site and upload your gift to the page.

✓ Create a thank-you message that includes the URL to the hidden page where readers can access your gift.

Notes

WAY 6

Give Readers a Sneak Peek at Your Book

One of the most effective gifts you can offer to your opt-in subscribers is a free chapter or two of your book. This tactic provides you with the opportunity to develop a relationship with your readers while providing them with a chance to preview what you have to offer.

Along with the free chapter or two, you can include other key components of your book. For example, your table of contents can serve as a mini sales letter, which can pique potential readers' interest. This approach will provide the reader with more information about you and your book and can further entice them to want to explore further and, thus, to purchase your book.

To prepare your free chapter giveaway, create an MS Word document that includes the following elements:

✓ Title page

✓ Foreword

✓ Table of contents

✓ Introduction

✓ About the author page

✓ Free chapter (or two)

✓ Marketing page inviting people to purchase your book

✓ Page footer with free giveaway document's page number, the title of your book, and the URL to your website

Save the Word document as a PDF file and upload it to your website. On that page, thank the reader for his or her interest in your book. Also, be sure to include the cover image of your book—along with instructions on how to download the free chapter(s).

Provide the PDF version of your giveaway

The reason you want to provide the PDF version, rather than the Word version, of your gift is because when people click to download the PDF file, it will open the file in their Web browser. If you upload the file as a Word document, your subscribers will receive a pop-up box requesting permission for the file to be downloaded to their computers—before they have a chance to preview the file. This request could scare off potential readers. Additionally, your content is better protected as a PDF file, rather than as an editable Word document.

Set up an opt-in form on your site with an auto-responder system like AWeber and invite people to enter their name and email address in exchange for a chapter of your book. (See Way 5 for details on how to set up your opt-in form and links to AWeber.) This opportunity will provide an easy way for you to send subscribers the link to your free chapter and provide you with the chance to begin building a relationship with them.

Action Step: Format a free chapter as a gift to your subscribers

✓ Copy the sections of your manuscript mentioned at the beginning of this "Way" and paste them into a fresh MS Word document.

✓ Format the footer section of the document to include your book title, your Web address (URL), and the giveaway document's page number. Then, save the file as a PDF.

✓ Add a marketing page that invites people to purchase your book.

Notes

_____

_____

_____

_____

_____

_____

_____

_____

_____

_____

_____

_____

_____

_____

_____

_____

_____

_____

_____

WAY 7

Develop Your Social Networking Presence

Social networking is a powerful way to grow your business, your reach, your readership, and, ultimately, your book sales. The purpose of social networking is not to promote your book constantly, but rather to network and build relationships. You want to be seen as someone who participates in and offers value to the community.

As an author, you want to become known for your area of expertise and as the go-to person on your topic. One way to demonstrate your knowledge is by joining social networking groups on topics of interest to your audience. Facebook and LinkedIn are great

43

social networks for authors, and both have active and responsive groups on just about any topic you can think of.

Once you've become a group member, you can join in the conversation, answer questions, and share ideas. You'll meet and connect with people and become known as an authority on your topic. Over time, you can let group members know about your book or your virtual book tour. They may even want to help promote your tour, as well as your book.

Brand your image across social networks

When joining social networks, you have the opportunity to fill out a profile page and add your photograph. By providing an attractive and professional photograph and taking the time to fill out your profile in detail, you'll make yourself more accessible and noticeable to your readers.

When uploading your photograph, choose an attractive, preferably professionally photographed, headshot photo. Use the same photograph on each of your social networking profiles, as this strategy will enhance your branding and people will come to recognize you.

Top four social networks for authors

As you know, there are seemingly countless social networks from which to choose. With this in mind, I'd like to recommend four of the top social networks for authors:

✓ Facebook (Facebook.com)

✓ LinkedIn (LinkedIn.com)

✓ Amazon Author Central (AuthorCentral.Amazon.com)

✓ Goodreads (Goodreads.com)

You may want to participate in all four of these networks, or you may want to take part in only one or two of them. You'll find details about each of these social networks in the following four Ways.

Action Step: Enhance your profile on social networks

✓ View your profiles on the social networks you frequent and make sure the information is current.

✓ Check to see that you're using an attractive headshot photo.

✓ Join a group or two on Facebook or LinkedIn on topics of interest to your readers. Ask questions and participate in discussions.

Notes

Create a Facebook Author Page

Facebook is currently considered to be the No. 1 social network in the world, with more than 618 million daily active users, as of December 2012. Having a presence on Facebook is important for an author, as it gives you more exposure and provides an effective way for your audience to connect with you.

On Facebook, you have the opportunity to create a page on any topic you'd like. For authors, having a Facebook author page provides you with opportunities to share your work and your book, as well as to connect with people interested in your topic.

A Facebook page can serve as an online community center where your readers come to find out more about your book and where they can interact with you.

Having a Facebook page provides an easy way for you to:

✓ Answer questions

✓ Announce and promote events

✓ Interact with your audience

Set up your author page

To set up your Facebook author page, scroll to the very bottom of the website at Facebook.com and click on the link to "create a page," search for "create a page" in the "Help" center.

From there, you'll be given a choice of categories. The "Author" category falls under the "Artist, Band, or Public Figure" tab.

As you set up your page, give strategic thought to what you want to call your page. As an author, using your name—or your name followed by the word "author"—provides you with a powerful branding opportunity.

You can brand your author page further by adding your photograph and uploading images related to your topic and book.

Get the conversation started

Once you have your branded author page set up, it's time to invite people to "like" your page and join in the conversation. Post a welcoming message and invite people to introduce themselves. You can also add conversation starters, polls, and questions to get the ball rolling. Before too long, people will be interacting with one another and starting new conversations.

Promote your author page on your blog, as well as on other social networks. You can add the URL to your author page in your email signature, as well as in your profile on each of your social networks. Your author page will become crucial to marketing for your virtual book tour.

Action Step: Create a Facebook author page

✓ Create an author page on Facebook and invite people to your page.

✓ Upload your headshot photograph and fill out the information about your page.

✓ Post a welcome message and invite people to introduce themselves.

✓ Reach out to your audience and invite them to "like" your author page.

Notes

9

Develop Your LinkedIn Presence

LinkedIn (LinkedIn.com) is a professional social network that provides you with the opportunity to interact with potentially millions of people across the globe. Your comprehensive profile can serve as an online resume, as you're provided with the opportunity to include your job experience, accomplishments, education, areas of expertise, and more. Take the time to add content to your LinkedIn profile as this will allow you to rank higher in LinkedIn's search engine and will increase the likelihood of people spending time reviewing your qualifications and experience.

Provide a strong headline on your profile

When filling out your profile, there's a field where you can provide a professional headline. Rather than listing a generic title like author, consider spicing up your headline to include keywords related to your industry. For example, relate to your genre or topic focus, as well as your formal accomplishments, such as "Best-selling Author of Children's Science Books."

Join groups that attract your target audience

LinkedIn provides one of the most interactive social networking group experiences. Since LinkedIn requires a high standard of integrity and has a low tolerance for spamming, the types of people who interact in LinkedIn groups are typically sincerely interested in the topic and networking with others.

By taking time to participate in group discussions, you can position yourself as an expert on your topic. This will allow you to develop relationships with people who may be interested in your book. Focus on answering questions and participating as a member of the community, rather than trying to sell your book or your programs. Build relationships first; the sales and referrals will follow.

Search for groups that your target market—or those that serve them—will be involved in. Join a few of these groups and their conversations. Even if you only visit your LinkedIn groups once a week, you'll grow your branding and expand your reach.

Become a group leader

You also have the opportunity to become a group leader. This prospect will further position you as an expert on your topic and provide you with relationship-building opportunities. As you select the topic for your group, give thought to your audience's interests. The purpose of your group is to provide your audience with a way to discuss subjects of interest to them. This is an opportunity for you to shine as an expert in your field.

Customizing your LinkedIn URL

When you join LinkedIn, you're assigned a random URL, which is not easy to remember. For branding purposes, you'll want to customize your LinkedIn URL. This distinction will add to your branding and make it easier for people to find you on LinkedIn. You can customize your URL from your profile page.

Action Step: Develop a LinkedIn presence

✓ Log into your LinkedIn account and update your profile with details about your experience, education, and areas of expertise.

✓ Update your headline to include descriptive keywords and create a custom LinkedIn URL.

✓ Do a search for groups centered on topics your audience is interested in, and join one or two that you plan on participating in at least once per week.

Notes

_____

_____

_____

_____

_____

_____

_____

_____

_____

_____

_____

_____

_____

_____

_____

_____

_____

_____

_____

WAY 10

Create and Enhance Your Amazon Author Central Page

Amazon Author Central is a free service provided by Amazon to allow authors to reach more readers, promote their books, and interact with the community. Having a well-developed author page on Amazon will provide you with increased visibility and access to more readers.

On Amazon Author Central you can:

✓ List your author biography

✓ Display your bibliography

✓ Post videos

✓ Highlight positive reviews of your book & add images

✓ Pull in your Twitter feed and your blog RSS feed

✓ Set up your custom Amazon Central URL

✓ Create opportunities for community interaction by initiating and participating in discussions

Set up your Amazon Author Central page

The first thing you'll want to do is set up your free Amazon Author Central account at AuthorCentral.Amazon.com. Next, add your photograph, biography, and books to your bibliography. (See my Amazon Author Central page at BooksByDvorah.com for an example.) For branding purposes, you may want to use the same professional photograph on Amazon as you use for your social networking profiles.

When adding your biography, keep it focused on your role as an author. List information that you most want your readers to know about you, your book, your work, and your journey as an author.

Add your Twitter feed and blog RSS feed

On your Author Central page, you'll easily be able to add your Twitter feed and the RSS feed from your blog. This free opportunity provides you with even more visibility and credibility, as readers will be able to view your Twitter stream and read excerpts of posts from your blog. Consequently, visitors to your author page will learn more about you and your work, and they may even visit your blog or follow you on Twitter.

Create events related to your book

You can easily list upcoming events, speaking engagements, book signings, and bookstore appearances on your Amazon Author Page. You can list both in-person and virtual events. For a virtual event, you'll want to enter the name of your event in the "Venue Name" field and "N/A" or "Online Event" in the "Address" fields. Also, you can list the URL and details about the event in the "Description" field. After you've created an event, it will be displayed in the scheduled events section on your profile page.

Add images and videos to your profile

It's very easy to add images and videos to your profile. Having an attractive and engaging profile will keep people on your author page longer and that extra browsing time will increase the likelihood of their purchasing your book or making contact with you.

Action Steps: Set up or update your profile on AuthorCentral.Amazon.com

✓ Register your author page.

✓ Add your author photo and bio.

✓ Add your Twitter feed and your blog's RSS feed.

✓ Upload images related to your book.

✓ Upload your video book trailer or a video about your book.

Notes

Join the Goodreads Author Program

Goodreads is a social network designed for authors and readers. This site has more than 4 million members and is considered to be the largest social network for readers. Goodreads members recommend books, create book lists, keep track of what they've read and would like to read, form groups and more.

To register for a Goodreads account, you simply enter your name and email address at Goodreads.com and select a password. You'll then be guided through a series of pages to help personalize your literary preferences. From there, you can update your profile, add your photograph, adjust your account settings, connect your Goodreads account to your Facebook account, and other choices.

Goodreads Author Program

As a published author who has registered as a member on Goodreads, you have the opportunity to join the Goodreads author program for free. This option will provide you with access to their promotional tools available to authors such as:

✓ Add a video book trailer to your profile

✓ List a book giveaway to generate buzz about your book

✓ Lead a Q&A discussion group for readers

To register for the Goodreads author program, do a search for your book on Goodreads.com. Click on your published author name or visit Goodreads.com/author/program. Scroll to the bottom of that page and click on "Is this you?" to send a request to join the Author Program. Within a few days, you'll receive email confirmation that your account has been upgraded to an author account. Joining the program merges your author page with your member page.

Participate in a Book Giveaway

Another way to get your book in front of more readers is to do a book giveaway on Goodreads. You decide how many physical copies of your book you'll give away and how long your contest will remain open. View book giveaways at Goodreads.com/giveaway to get ideas for your own book giveaway. This promotion will get a lot of attention for your book, as well as potential purchases. It's common to have hundreds of people enter book giveaway contests.

You can get additional traffic to your book giveaway page by promoting your contest on social networks and your blog. You can also reach out or send announcements to your friends on Goodreads. Readers simply click to enter the contest. At the end of the contest period, Goodreads automatically selects the winners with a random-number generator.

Once the winners are selected, you're required to mail each one a physical copy of your book. To make the most of this opportunity, you may want to sign each book and include a bookmark or postcard that invites your readers to connect with you.

Action Steps: Register for a Goodreads account and join the Author Program

✓ Register as a member on Goodreads and fill out your profile in detail.

✓ Add your photograph.

✓ Create a recommended reading list.

✓ Register for the Goodreads author program.

Notes

WAY 12

Line Up Your Tour Hosts

Now it's time to set the destinations for your virtual book tour. Lining up tour hosts is easier than it may seem, and this exercise provides you with fantastic opportunities for building and strengthening relationships with colleagues and leaders in your industry.

When considering potential virtual book tour hosts, take into account the following:

✓ Do they have an attractive blog?

✓ Is their blog up-to-date, with new content being added regularly?

✓ Is the topic of their blog of interest to your target audience?

63

Whom do you know?

The fastest and easiest way to line up hosts for your virtual book tour is to contact blog owners you know who write on issues related to the topic of your book. You already have a relationship with them, and it's likely they trust and respect you and know that the topic you write on will be of interest to their readers.

Blog search engines

Another way you can find blog hosts is to locate blogs on your topic via blog search engines. Technorati.com is one of the most popular blog search engines. Google Blog Search is another (Google.com/blogsearch). You simply type in keywords related to your topic and you'll be provided with a list of blogs. You can then visit these blogs to decide if you'd like to reach out to the blog owners.

Blogs as mini search engines

You can also locate potential tour hosts by visiting blogs that are featured on blogs in your niche. When you get to each site, take a look on the blog's sidebar to see if there are recommended sites. Also check the blog posts to see if there are guest bloggers. If so, visit those blogs to see if they meet your book tour criteria. If they do, you can reach out to those additional blog owners.

Blog owners appreciate visitors and many welcome guest bloggers

By promoting your virtual book tour, you'll be driving new traffic to each blog on your tour. Blog owners are thrilled to have more people visiting their sites, and their readers will appreciate having access to your relevant content. When you reach out to potential tour hosts, let them know you'll be conducting a virtual book tour and that you'd love to feature their blog on your tour.

Action Step: Create a list of potential virtual book tour hosts

On a fresh sheet of paper, jot down the answers to the following questions:

- ✓ What's the topic or area of focus for your book?

- ✓ What are your ideal readers interested in?

- ✓ Whom do you know with a blog that focuses on topics of interest to your ideal reader?

- ✓ Which blogs in your niche would you love to be featured on, but you don't personally know the blog owner?

- ✓ Whom do you know who may be a good contact for the owners of the blogs where you'd love to be featured?

Notes

WAY 13

Share Your Appreciation

Once you've lined up your tour hosts, you'll want to thank them. In our fast-paced world, taking the time to express appreciation is noticed and goes a long way toward strengthening relationships.

During your virtual book tour, you can show your appreciation in a variety of ways. In addition to sending an email thanking your hosts, and confirming tour dates, there are several effective ways to share your appreciation.

I also highly recommend you check out the book *Thank You Power* by Deborah Norville.

Send your hosts a copy of your book

Send all of your hosts a copy of your book in their preferred format. Ask them if they'd prefer a digital version or a print copy. This option will provide them with easy access to your topic, and they will be able to more easily promote your work. Most importantly, your relationship with them will be strengthened, as they likely will appreciate your gesture.

Thank your hosts on your blog

Another way to share your appreciation is to mention each of your hosts in a dedicated blog post, to be featured on your site.

For example, each morning of your tour, compose a blog post letting your readers know where you're traveling and what you'll be sharing. As part of this blog post, you can mention the blog owner's name, the URL to your post on their site, and a comment or sentence about his or her area of expertise.

Thank all hosts on their blogs

In addition to mentioning your hosts on blog posts published on **your** blog, you can begin each guest blog post, which will be featured by your tour hosts, by thanking that day's host for hosting you on your virtual book tour.

Take time to send a handwritten card

How do you feel when you receive a heartfelt note of appreciation through the mail? As part of your virtual book tour, make it a practice to send your tour hosts handwritten greeting cards, thanking them and letting them know you appreciate their participation.

Consider sending this card as soon as they've agreed to be a tour host. This will further ensure their participation and the likelihood that they'll more readily promote your book tour. People love receiving handwritten greeting cards. They're likely to keep them and display them on their desks.

The easiest way to streamline your card sending is to use a service such as SendOutCards, which allows you to create your customized greeting card online (CardsYouRemember.com). You can add a personalized note and they print and send your cards for you, through the mail, with a stamp.

Action Step: Create a tracking sheet to monitor your appreciation activity

Create a tracking form in Microsoft Word or in Microsoft Excel so you can keep track of activities:

✓ Thank-you emails sent and Thank-you cards sent.

✓ Type of book sent (digital or print version.)

✓ Daily post letting readers know where you'll be.

✓ Visit to each tour stop to leave a comment thanking your hosts.

69

Notes

WAY 14

Create Content for Your Virtual Book Tour

One of the primary activities of a virtual book tour is sharing articles as a guest blogger on blogs that attract your target audience. Guest blogging is a powerful way for you to become known for your expertise and is an effective tool for growing relationships.

Blog owners are constantly creating and looking for fresh content for their blogs. By offering to be a guest blogger, you're creating a win/win/win situation. You benefit by being endorsed by the blog owner and being discovered by new readers; the blog owner benefits by having relevant, fresh content for his or her site; and the readers benefit by having access to new information and ideas on topics of interest to them.

In Way 15 you'll find suggestions for blog topics and ideas. In the meantime, check out the book *Content Rules* by Ann Handley and C.C. Chapman.

Multimedia blog posts

In addition to written articles, your blog posts can consist of audio and video recordings. You can share audio interviews and book talks, as well as video tips, book excerpts, and more. In Way 17 you'll learn more about creating audios and in Way 18 you'll learn more about creating videos.

Create content ahead of time

Schedule time to create your book tour content before your tour begins. This strategy will allow you to segment your activities and enjoy your book tour when it takes place. For example, you may want to dedicate one or two weeks to write your articles and another week or two to record your audio and video presentations and interviews.

You can send your post to each host ahead of time. They can then schedule your post to be published on the agreed-upon date and provide you with the URL to where your post will appear on that date. You can save this URL in a Word document or Excel spreadsheet for easy access.

By having your hosts schedule your posts ahead of time, you'll be assured that everything is all set. However, you may want to send a courtesy email to your hosts the day before you'll be traveling to their site. This will remind them to promote your tour and will provide you with another opportunity to thank them.

Action Step: Develop a Content Creation Plan of Action

✓ Create a virtual book tour calendar and block out a week or two for creating written content for your blog posts.

✓ If you'll be adding a multimedia component to your tour, map out a week or two for creating audio and video content.

✓ Create an Word document or Excel spreadsheet where you can easily store your virtual book tour dates and the URLs to where your posts will be showing up each day.

Notes

WAY 15

Things to Blog about During Your Book Tour

As you prepare for your virtual book tour, you may be wondering how you're going to come up with enough ideas to create content for each day of your tour. In this Way, you'll be provided with several logical, as well as some out-of-the-box, suggestions to help stimulate ideas.

Each of your blog posts should be unique and fresh, since you don't want the same article to appear on more than one site during your book tour. Start with the book *So You Want to Write a Guest Post* by Jaime McDougall and read on for more ideas.

Share your story

The focus of your virtual book tour is on you and your book. Your readers will be interested in hearing about your journey as an author and how it is that you decided to write on your chosen topic. Share this information with them in the form of stories. You can present these stories in written, audio, or video format. People love stories and letting them "peek behind the curtain" to get to know you will deepen their connection to you.

Written author interviews

Written interviews, where you, the author, address a series of questions, will provide a compelling format for blog posts. One interview can focus on your journey as an author, while another interview focuses on how you came to write a book on this topic.

Share book excerpts

As part of your book tour, you may want to share excerpts from your book. However, before doing so, be sure to check with your publisher to make sure you retain the rights to do so. You can share a stand-alone section of your book, or you can add introductory comments regarding the excerpt you're about to share.

Talk about your topic

Your book is on a topic about which you're passionate. In addition to sharing excerpts of your book, write about your topic. Provide thought-provoking content to stimulate your readers' minds.

One way to come up with ten blog posts on your topic is to create a bulleted list of the top ten questions your audience has or the top ten things they need to know about your topic. This list will provide you with the foundation for ten articles that can be shared as written, audio, or video blog posts.

You can take your guest blog posts one step further and repurpose them into another book. See Way 20 and the book *How to Blog a Book* by Nina Amir for more ideas.

Action Step: Compose a list of potential titles for your blog posts

✓ List the top ten most common questions people ask on your topic.

✓ List ten questions you can answer about your journey as an author.

✓ List topics you'd like to include as part of your virtual book tour.

✓ Review these lists and begin to compose compelling, keyword rich, blog post titles.

Notes

16

Make the Most of Your Blog Posts

In essence, your audio, video, and written blog posts are "virtual real estate." In addition to providing informational, educational, or entertaining content, you can include subtle marketing material.

For example, at the end of each of your blog posts, you can include information about yourself along with a compelling reason why people should come to your blog.

Respond to readers' comments

During your virtual book tour, people will share comments and ask questions. Use this interaction as an opportunity to both illustrate your expertise and build a relationship with your readers.

One way to encourage comments is to ask a question at the end of your blog posts. For example, you can ask the readers' opinion of what you wrote or a specific question. Then respond to their opinions. Authors who respond to comments generally get many more comments than those who don't. This in turn helps with search engine optimization (SEO).

During your virtual book tour, you'll want to visit each blog multiple times: at least once on the day you're scheduled to appear there, as well as throughout the tour. These visits will allow you to respond to additional comments.

Add images to your blog posts

Adding images to your blog posts makes them more attractive and engages your readers. Such images will increase the likelihood of people reading through your post and possibly asking a question or sharing a comment. Adding images also makes it easier for people to share your post on Pinterest, thus broadening your reach.

Be sure to include a photograph of you smiling with each blog post, as well as an image of your book. These additional steps will grow your branding and allow your readers to identify with you.

Create a Call to Action in your post signature

As part of your book tour, you'll have the opportunity to build relationships with new readers. Include a call to action in the signature block at the end of each blog post. An example of an effective call to action is an invitation to readers to visit your blog where they can enter their names and email addresses in order to receive a free chapter of your book.

Create a signature template file

Create a template file you can use for each of your posts. Open up a Word document and compose your blog post signature. Typically, this signature block includes 100–150 words and can incorporate things like your name, credentials, book title, blog URL, how you help people, and a compelling reason why people should visit your blog. Offering people a free chapter of your book is an excellent strategy.

Save this document so you can easily copy and paste the content to the bottom of each of your blog posts.

Action Step: Create Your Blog Post Signature File

✓ Create a new folder on your computer where you can keep all of the files on your virtual book tour.

✓ Design a compelling signature template file for your blog posts. Include your author photograph and book cover along with a compelling reason why people should visit your blog.

✓ Save your signature file in your virtual book tour folder.

Notes

WAY 17

Participate in Audio Interviews

An author interview provides compelling content and helps you promote your book and brand. Participating in audio interviews is a powerful way to create content and a way to provide for your audience to hear your voice and connect with you. In addition to your live audio interviews, the recordings can be made available for people to listen to.

Practice Interview session

The best way to "get your feet wet" is to have someone you know interview you and record that session. Treat it as if there are a hundred people on the line. This experience will prove to be invaluable because you can critique your own performance and it will provide you with an interview recording you can use as part of your virtual book tour. 83

Arrange for some of your tour hosts to interview you

In addition to your practice interview session, you may want to have some of your virtual book tour hosts interview you. Such opportunities will provide you with additional multimedia content and raise your level of credibility.

Prepare for your interviews

To prepare for your interviews, compose a list of the top ten questions your audience would most like to know about you, your book, or your topic. These items will serve as the foundation of your audio interviews.

Sample interview questions

In addition to the list of questions you've composed, here are some additional ideas:

For Fiction Books

✓ Who are the characters in the book?

✓ Why did you choose those particular characters?

✓ What is the premise of the story?

For Nonfiction Books

✓ How did you get interested in this topic?

✓ What would you like readers to walk away with after reading your book?

✓ Why did you decide to write a book on this topic?

Have your recording transcribed and repurpose the content

Repurposing is the act of creating content once and reformatting it to be used in a wide variety of channels. Once you've recorded your interview, have it transcribed and distribute that written content in different formats. For example, you can create blog posts or a free report to offer to your opt-in subscribers. See Way 20 for more on repurposing your content.

Action Steps: Prepare for and Participate in an Audio Interview

✓ Register for a free tele-conferencing account with FreeConferenceCalling.com or FreeConferenceCall.com or a trial account with InstantTeleseminar.com

✓ Schedule a time for a relative, friend, or colleague to interview you.

✓ Compose a list of ten questions you'd like to be asked during your interview.

✓ Dial in to your conference call line, initiate the recording, and answer each question with as much detail as possible.

✓ Have the interview transcribed and divide it up to use for blog posts or articles, or use it in its entirety as a special report.

Notes

WAY 18

Create Videos as Part of Your Book Tour

Video adds a compelling component to your virtual book tour. It provides a way for people to both connect with you and find out more about you and your book "in living color." You can create a simple "talking head" type of video by turning on your webcam and speaking into the camera. You can offer book readings or create how-to videos by recording a PowerPoint presentation or making a screen-capture video using content on your computer screen.

Types of videos

The three most popular formats for online video are talking head, screen capture, and PowerPoint.

87

Talking Head videos

Talking head videos are where you create a video with a webcam or video camera. You can sit at your desk, turn on your webcam or video camera, and begin speaking. This video format is fast, easy, affordable, and effective. A talking head video allows your audience to both see and hear you, and it's a powerful relationship-building tool.

Screen-Capture video

Another type of video is called screen-capture video. This is where you create videos from content that's on your computer screen. You can record a live Webinar, take readers on a tour of a website, explain a software program, and much more.

PowerPoint video

With a PowerPoint video, you share text and images in a PowerPoint presentation. To record this video, you can either use the video recorder included in Microsoft PowerPoint 2007 and higher, or you can use a screen-capture video program.

The most popular screen-capture video programs are Jing Project (JingProject.com) and Camtasia Studio (CamtasiaStudio.com). Both programs are created by Tech Smith. Jing Project allows you to record videos up to five minutes in length while there is no time limitation with Camtasia Studio.

Additional video ideas

In addition to the above recommendations, here's a suggested list of video-creation ideas:

Read a chapter of your book aloud. You can even record each of your chapters and create a video book (be sure to check with your publisher to make sure you are not violating your publishing agreement in doing this). You can capture this as a talking head video or as a PowerPoint video.

✓ Record a video of a live book signing or a book talk.

✓ Conduct an interview and record it with a video camera.

Share your videos on the Internet

One of the easiest ways to share your videos on the Internet is by uploading them to YouTube. It's easy to set up an account and simple to upload a video. When you set up and login to your YouTube account, you'll have easy access to the upload feature. Currently that option is located to the left of your YouTube username, at the top right of your screen.

Once you've uploaded your video, you can click on the share tab to access the URL or embed code to your video. You can share the URL with your social networks and you can create a video post and embed the video code to your blog.

Action Steps: Produce a Web video and upload it to YouTube

✓ Register for a free Jing Project account.

✓ Download and install the Jing Project software.

✓ Look into getting Camtasia Studio.

✓ Record a PowerPoint presentation, screen-capture video, or talking head video.

✓ Upload your video to YouTube.

WAY 19

Keep Organized

There are many components of a virtual book tour and much to keep track of. You want to have an easy way to monitor your virtual book tour details and have everything easily accessible. Staying organized will allow for a smooth-running and enjoyable event.

Create an Excel spreadsheet

Having the details of your book tour in a spreadsheet will help you to keep organized. With the click of your mouse, you'll be able to verify which tasks you've completed.

In Way 12 we talked about techniques to line up your book tour hosts. You'll want to set up a tracking sheet that lists which site you're traveling to on which date, along with the name and contact information of the blog owner. This tactic will make it easy to see which dates you have open so you can fill up your virtual book tour schedule without double-booking yourself.

Here's a list of activities you'll want to keep track of:

✓ Which blog you're traveling to on what date

✓ That you've given each host your blog post, headshot photo, and book image

✓ That you've sent your host a copy of your book

✓ That you've sent your host a thank-you card

✓ The URL where each post will appear on each host's blog

✓ That you've posted a blog comment on your guest post, thanking your host

✓ That you've returned to each blog to respond to comments

Create a virtual book tour schedule page on your blog

By posting your virtual book tour schedule on your blog, you can direct people to that page and have one handy location where people can access all the stops on your tour. List the date and title of your blog post for each day of your tour.

Wait until your post has been published to add the hyperlink to a tour destination. Take note that the URLs to your blog posts will not be valid until the day they're published. Until that time, the URL will lead to an error page. You may want to post a note at the top of your schedule letting people know that each morning of the dates listed, the URL to that tour stop will be posted.

Action Step: Get organized!

As you prepare for your virtual book tour, you'll want to make sure you're well organized and that you have your systems in place.

✓ Create a spreadsheet and add columns for each of the above mentioned virtual book tour activities.

✓ Create a virtual book tour schedule page on your blog, and save it in draft mode until you are ready to publish it.

✓ Plug your virtual book tour schedule into your main business calendar.

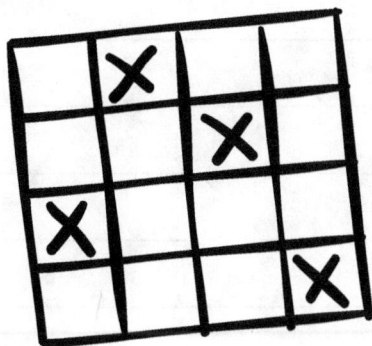

Notes

Repurpose Your Virtual Book Tour Content

As mentioned in Way 17, repurposing is the act of creating content once, and repurposing it into a wide variety of formats. This repurposed material can be used as content for your virtual book tour as well as for gifts that you offer subscribers to your email list. Additionally, repurposed content can be used when creating courses or products that you sell.

Repurposing your content allows you to provide your audience with material in the medium they most enjoy and that complements their learning style. Some people prefer to read, while others like to listen to audio recordings, and still others prefer to view videos. Why not provide content in all of these formats and give people a range of options to choose from?

Create an eBook or guide with your virtual book tour content

Throughout the course of your virtual book tour, you'll have created a rich supply of new content that you can repurpose. Compiling your blog posts into one document to create an eBook or guide to your book tour would make an impressive gift to your email subscribers or purchasers of your book. This collection of blog posts could even be sold as a stand-alone product.

As you complete each blog post, in addition to saving it as a file in your virtual book tour folder on your computer, paste a copy into a Word document to create a compilation of all of your blog posts. You can add a title page, about the author page, a footer with page numbers and the URL to your website, and a table of contents. You can also add a marketing page where you invite your readers to purchase your book. To further engage your readers, be sure to add images to your document.

Your blog posts that provide audio and video content can also be included in this master document. You can do this by listing the title of your audio or video blog post as well as a written description of what is discussed in the audio or video. You can even include a screen capture image of your audio or video player along with a hyperlink to your multimedia content. That way when people click on the hyperlinked image they will be able to access your audio or video.

When you're ready to prepare your master document to share with others, be sure to have it carefully proofread. Once you're satisfied that this file is ready to share with the world, save it in PDF format. This will make it easier for your audience to access and will add a layer of protection to your content.

Repurposing your virtual book tour content makes a beautiful memento and provides additional opportunities to reach your audience.

Action Step: Repurpose Your Virtual Book Tour Content

✓ Create a master document where you can paste a copy of each blog post from your virtual book tour.

✓ Format your document to include the items outlined in this "Way".

✓ Gift thought to whether you will offer this as a gift or sell as a product.

Notes

21

Promote Your Virtual Book Tour

Now that you're organized and have your systems in place, it's time to begin promoting your virtual book tour. Have each tour host announce to their subscribers the date you'll be traveling to their site as well as announce your guest appearance to their followers on social networks.

Post to your blog each day of your tour

One way to gain momentum and create excitement about your book tour is for you to write a brief blog post on your site letting people know where you'll be each day. You can then publish an announcement on Twitter and Facebook about that day's blog post.

This post can be brief and include the name and URL to that day's tour site—along with the topic you'll be speaking about. You may want to include a few sentences about that day's post and then let your readers know they can view the rest of the article by clicking on the URL.

Sign up for Gravatar

When registering to post a blog comment, you have the opportunity to list your blog URL. You'll notice that when your comment goes live, your name is hyperlinked. When anyone clicks on your name, it will take him or her to your blog.

Register your email address and upload a headshot photo at Gravatar.com. Then, when you post a blog comment using that email address anywhere on the Internet, your photo will show up.

Create buzz about your virtual book tour

During your book tour, you'll want to find ways to create buzz. The most effective way to do this is to post announcements on social networks and have your followers help spread the word.

Create a Facebook page or a Facebook event specifically for your virtual book tour so people can read the exciting comments and announcements at one central location. Alternatively, you can use your Facebook author page to promote your tour.

Ask for book reviews

You can also create buzz by having readers share a brief review or testimonial about your book. They can publish this as a review on your book's Amazon listing as well as to your blog or Facebook page.

Ask for reviews as many of your readers will want to help promote your book.

Action Step: Promote your virtual book tour

✓ Create a Facebook page or a Facebook event, to promote your tour (See Way 8, Facebook.com/pages, Facebook.com/events/list).

✓ Register for an account at Gravatar.com so your photograph shows up when you leave blog comments.

✓ Encourage your readers to comment on your guest blog posts and to send out a tweet or Facebook message to share your posts with others.

✓ Ask for book reviews.

Notes

Notes

Conclusion

Now that you've gone through this guide once, go through again and reread your notes and highlighted passages. Review your virtual book tour notebook where you've kept track of your action steps.

Take a deep breath, and, if you haven't yet done so, get out your calendar and schedule your virtual book tour.

By *choosing to act* on what you've learned in this guide, you'll be able to grow your readership while taking your book on tour around the globe—without leaving home. Have fun with this golden opportunity and **do something to promote your virtual book tour each day**.

About D'vorah

D'vorah Lansky, M.Ed. is the bestselling author of several books including; the *Action Guides for Authors* series of workbooks and journals.

Since 2007 D'vorah has created more than 25, successful, online programs and has taught and coached thousands of authors across the globe.

She specializes in teaching authors how to build a business around their books, as they grow their reach and share their message with the world.

To view all of D'vorah's books visit her on Amazon at: BooksByDvorah.com

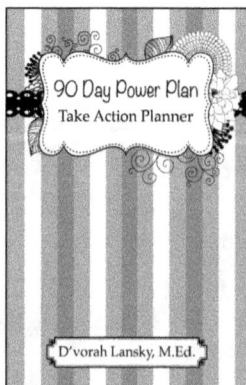

D'VORAH LANSKY

Book Marketing Made Easy

Simple Strategies for Selling Your Nonfiction Book Online

90 Day Power Plan
Take Action Planner

D'vorah Lansky, M.Ed.

A Gift from D'vorah

Profit Beyond Your Book Sales as you Create a Challenge Experience Based on Your Knowledge

I have an action guide for you that will help you:

Discover how to design the perfect learning experience for your ideal students, clients, and customers!

In this action guide, you'll access worksheets and checklists to help you:

📖 Grow your business and your reach while doing what you enjoy most!

📖 Expand your visibility and your credibility by sharing your knowledge and expertise!

📖 Apply a step-by-step formula for creating an effective online training program!

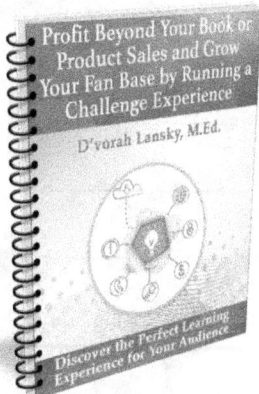

Profit Beyond Your Book or Product Sales and Grow Your Fan Base by Running a Challenge Experience

D'vorah Lansky, M.Ed.

Discover the Perfect Learning Experience for Your Audience

Go here to claim your gift:
ShareYourBrilliance.com/gift

Notes

Notes

Notes

Notes

Praise for *21 Ways to Launch a Successful Virtual Book Tour*

"Gaining visibility is essential for authors. One of the best ways to gain visibility today is via the Internet, and one of the best ways to gain visibility on the Internet is via a virtual book tour. D'vorah Lansky's *21 Ways to Launch a Successful Virtual Book Tour* walks you through the process of embarking on a virtual book tour for your book. She provides a series of simple—yet extremely effective—strategies for getting your book and your message in front of thousands of new readers. Pick up a copy of this gem today and get ready to take your book on tour globally—without leaving home! There is no better way to be seen as relevant, current, consistent and everywhere!"

David L. Hancock, founder of Morgan James Publishing and
co-author of *The Entrepreneurial Author*, Morgan-James.com

"A virtual book tour has many moving parts; but with D'vorah Lansky's knowledgeable and experienced guidance in this book, authors will be able to plan their own tours—and do it with great confidence and success."

Sandra Beckwith, publisher of *Build Book Buzz* and author of *Get Your Book in the News: How to Write a Press Release That Announces Your Book*, BuildBookBuzz.com

"In an age when rising above all the clutter and noise online seems increasingly difficult, D'vorah Lansky blazes a trail to *real* results that any book or eBook author can follow with confidence. A well-executed, virtual book tour rates as the No. 1 way to get exposure, build credibility, attract readers, and develop relationships with movers and shakers in a niche—all at the same time! If you want to launch a successful virtual book tour, I know of no better teacher than D'vorah. Do yourself a favor, follow her instructions to the letter, and reap the massive rewards every book author craves."

Jim Edwards, eBook Marketing Pioneer and author of *How To Write and Publish Your Own eBook . . . in as little as 7 Days, v2.0*, 7dayebook.com

"Virtual book tours help authors showcase their books to a broad audience of targeted consumers across key social-media marketing channels. A well-organized, virtual book tour campaign benefits authors by increasing exposure, credibility, authority, and influence. D'vorah offers great strategies and tactics on every aspect of structuring and building an effective and well-organized virtual book tour campaign that will help authors maximize efficiency and effectiveness."

Jo Ann Kairys, award-winning author of *Sunbelievable: A Children's Picture Book*
StoryQuestBooks.com

"Getting readers for your book is getting tougher and tougher. Even more difficult is attracting enough interested people to attend your book signing at a local bookstore. And with all the techie tools that you can use to promote your book, you can get overwhelmed trying to decide just what to use to get attention. D'vorah Lansky peels back the curtain on what a virtual book tour is, how to use it to sell more books to get more readers, and how to develop multiple streams of income. Not based solely in theory, D'vorah's methods have helped her clients go from unknown to well-known authors using a well-planned, virtual book tour. Get your message in front of a willing audience by digesting *21 Ways to Launch a Successful Virtual Book Tour,* so you can easily cut through the literary clutter."

Leesa Barnes, a leading authority on virtual events
VirtualEventAlliance.com

"D'vorah is *the*'Virtual Book Tour Master.'She has helped her students and clients launch hugely successful virtual book tours! She is a naturally gifted teacher with an ability to quickly make complex topics easy to digest. D'vorah's training content is top notch and always delivered with precision and excellence."

Craig Cannings, co-founder of the VAClassroom
VAClassroom.com

"D'vorah Lansky is a book-marketing guru with advice to help authors at every level of experience. Her latest book, *21 Ways to Launch a Successful Virtual Book Tour*, is packed with tips for making the most of online opportunities—from virtual book tours to author interviews and everything in between. D'vorah explains it all in this easy to read guide, sure to give any writer a boost in ideas and direction. Highly recommended."

Jason Matthews, author of novels and how-to guides for self-publishing
TheLittleUniverse.com

"Gone are the days when authors need to board an aircraft to promote their books. The Internet has created a world of opportunities for authors, including the possibility of taking their books across borders. D'vorah demonstrates a keen understanding of the nuances of a virtual book tour. I highly recommend D'vorah for her knowledge and understanding of virtual book tours."

Eunice Nisbett, owner of Savvy Book Marketing
SavvyVirtuals.co/bookmarketing